Memoirs
of
Desire
(Our Family Tree)

Ashley Anderson

Memoirs of Desire
Published by Kingdom Publishing, LLC
Odenton, MD 21113

Printed in the U.S.A.

ISBN: 978-1-947741-71-3

Scripture quotations noted AMPLIFIED or AMP are taken from the the Amplified® Bible, copyright © 1954, 1958, 1962, 1964, 1965, 1987 by The Lockman Foundation. Used by permission (www.Lockman.org).

Cover design by Antonio Palmer

Photography by Joyce Images, LLC

Dedication

I dedicate this book to all the people out there who are afraid to use their voice. Remember, you are not alone.

Table of Contents

Introduction

"The earnest (heart-felt, continued) prayer of a righteous man makes tremendous power available [dynamic in its working]."
James 5:16 (AMP)

Mental health is a real problem in my community. Sadly, resources for mental health issues are not always common knowledge to the people living through them. Because of this, many people dealing with mental health issues have ended up incarcerated. Studies have shown that 25% of prisoners suffer from some form of mental illness; It's amazing how we don't see this as a problem.

Through reading this story, I hope you feel more comfortable opening up about past traumas and experiences like mine. I'm confident that a lot of you will find it highly relatable.

If you know of anyone that may be crying out for help, please help them. You never know what type of impact you may have on someone's life.

On your journey through this book series, I'll show you where I started, how I got through, and how to move forward. Never let your past define who you are in a world full of possibilities.

Memoirs of Desire

Chapter 1
The Coldest Winter Ever

It was a cold winter morning in December of 2014. There I was at the age of 27 with the finest things. The finest car, nice shoes, and great clothes. I reflected on the fact that everyone around me believed that they really knew me. Many even envied me and developed jealousy. People truly enjoyed my company and thought my life was altogether different than what it really was. The truth of the matter is no one really knew me. I was just covering up the pain I felt far beyond the surface.

Behind the public façade lived a 4-year-old little girl who grew up far before her time. Truthfully, my life was in shambles. Everyone thought I had it made but didn't know my daily struggles with my past. This lifestyle suppressed the truth and buried it deep within me.

Behind that beautiful smile lived a 4-year-old girl yearning to be loved and protected by her family. This 4-year-old girl had a 14-year-old mother who was searching for love in all the wrong places.

My mother was a child herself, craving the love, affection, and attention of countless men who were far from the epitome of a father.

When you have a child, they are a vessel directly from you. While my mom was busy trying to grow up, she gave birth to a young precious baby girl that needed her love, attention, affection, and protection.

My mother was trying to escape her own pain, trauma, abuse, and past misfortune. Behind that 14-year-old girl lived an 11-year-old girl who was constantly molested by a close family member.

Not only did this family member molest my mother, but they gave her drugs continuously. I couldn't imagine the hurt and loneliness of not feeling protected at such a young age... would you be able to not say anything, time after time? My mother suppressed this trauma deep within herself.

She felt ashamed; this surely couldn't be mentioned within the family. These were times when abuse was given but not told within the family, and hidden from other family members, and most importantly hidden from outsiders.
My mother was stripped of her innocence at such a young age.

She missed out on her wonderful teenage years and skipped over to playing house. This 14-year-old little girl's fairy tale world became a broken reality. I can't imagine how scared my mother had to be experiencing such abuse...can you? This abuse continued for years and everyone kept quiet about it like it was normal.

There was nothing normal about my mothers' family member abusing her, but again she believed in keeping quiet about such trauma within the family.

Grandma knew nothing. My grandmother was thinking, maybe my daughter is just going through some growing pains as a young woman. "Maybe she is just confused from all the abuse, so I allowed her to see her dad." (See how the cycle continues).

I knew my granddad, but I knew him as what they called "a bum". He lived right in front of Lexington Market where all the homeless people slept. As a child, I remember my grandmother going to look for him to make sure he had food and money because he had lost his mind from taking speed to keep him going at his DJ gigs.

My mother was holding all this in just to make my grandmother happy because she didn't want her to worry. After all, she worked hard and already had endured so much. No, she could never bother her about the disgraceful things going on behind her back, especially because the one doing all the hurt was her mom's best friend and family member. "It would hurt mommy if I said something".

But there she was, 14 years old with a new baby which is in turn grandma's baby. Mothers tending to grandchildren as if they gave birth to them is extremely common in the black community and my grandmother was not exempt from this. As the baby grew, mommy's drug habit started getting out of control. She began to get with any man who would brake whatever innocence she had left, transforming a sweet young girl to an addicted young woman.

You see, grandma couldn't help much because she always wanted a future for her young family. With continued education tying up her income, she didn't have much financial support to give. Four long years and mommy's addiction became like a raging bull, but it seemed more like a thief in the night for her. She hooked up with a young fella who she thought could change all that.

Chapter 2
Momma's Prize

Sweet on the eyes and handsome, all the ladies wanted him. She fell in love and 6 months later, momma was pregnant again. Grandma couldn't help much on top of working 7pm-11am, school until six, and then work again. How did mom make this work? She shacked up because she felt like this was the man of her dreams, "Oh he's everything". Then, came Jr. He was the cutest little guy you've ever seen. Meanwhile, snort here…smoke there… "I won't get addicted". Unfortunately, this time it was something that would alter her mind and tear her world apart. She manufactured the idea of happiness in her obsession. Crack cocaine is a major thing that destroys families generation after generation. So now, her newborn baby was not getting any attention and hardly eating. I was just 5 years old at that time, trying my best to raise my baby brother, after all, I did love to play with dolls.

My mom would use anything that could give her that high. She had become a product of the abuse she experienced. The drugs had become so addictive that she just couldn't shake it. Bills stopped getting paid to keep up with the habit and not much later there was an eviction notice on our door. I've always wondered why someone would come and put your family's belongings out on the streets, "why would they do this to us?" I believe that in that moment doubt was created in me along with a distrust for people. Thankfully, God sends angels that you don't always recognize!

Chapter 3

The Gift and The Curse

My grandmother, what a blessing she has always been. She got us a little apartment because the streets were no place for a family with young children. Meanwhile, she was still striving to finish school to become the RN she always dreamt of being while working as an LPN. In her mind she knew she needed to help us and honestly, now looking back I think that is what kept her going. She gave us this gift but in a matter of months that home became a war zone and a child's nightmare. Fighting and abuse became a normal sight to us at just 6 and 2 years old. I can always remember the times when I watched them getting high. I had a feeling that things would never be the same.

I automatically started feeling like I had to protect my little brother, the baby, and funny I was a baby myself. One day the fighting was so bad that our neighbors stepped in. This was a time when people cared about what was right or wrong. The neighbors stepping in resulted in my stepfather being locked up and I was relieved! The beatings stopped, the fighting calmed down, but the drugs…the drugs were a more powerful thing.

As for the lost, 19-year-old, single mother, she would still do anything to satisfy her high even if it meant her children didn't eat. For days my brother and I ate peanut butter sandwiches. The peanut butter with the pig on the can. We were satisfied, we had no choice. Until one night mommy had no money and our public assistance came through. She took all the food and left.

We were so hungry. The only thing I was worried about at that time was my little brother eating. He was crying so bad that I fed him paint chips so that he would feel full. Now looking back, I don't know why that was my choice. I was 6 years old what else was I to do? My brother was later diagnosed with lead paint poisoning.

As I am sitting here typing this, I feel incredibly bad. If only I could have done something differently.

My stepfather finally got released from prison. Low and behold there was food in the house again and with it came the fighting and the beatings. I remember one night, my mother and stepfather fought so bad that they left my brother and I sitting on the sidewalk on Liberty heights and Garrison in Baltimore. I picked my brother up and just started walking with not even an inch of fear in my heart. I don't know what sparked in my mom but she came and found us. I knew she would come to rescue us.

Chapter 4

The Guiding Guardian Angel

My grandmother was still working on succeeding. Still, she always came through on paying our bills and even furnished our home. Eventually, we got evicted from our second home. She came to pick up our things only to arrive and find out they were already sold. She was so hurt. My little brother was in his "growing years", he didn't smile much and always seemed so sad. As I look back over the years, I always wanted to fix his pain. I knew he deserved so much better.

Daddy was locked up again and the drugs completely destroyed our little family. Mommy was looking for peace, her innocence, and acceptance which she no longer looked for in people but found it in drugs. My brother and I were 8 and 4 years old still outside at 11:00pm. When all my friends went in, I wondered why no one was looking for us. It wasn't all bad and whatever my mom was doing in the streets, she made sure no one did anything to us.

Memoirs of Desire

Chapter 5
Mental Mentality

After years of this it was our normal way of living. We were raising ourselves, daddy stayed locked up, and my mom was always at the races when he was gone. One day things took a turn for the worst. I know you are thinking, how could it get any worse? But it did! Now mommy started seeing things on the roof and often heard voices under the bed of people who really weren't there. I mean, can you imagine hearing people that aren't there? Often, when I came home, mommy wanted to know if I was touched by a man. SHE SCARED THE LIVING SHIT OUT OF ME.

I can remember sitting up all night just so she wouldn't get high or leave. Because I was up, she began to take me with her to purchase the drugs. This kind of behavior went on for years. I remember one time when she needed to use, she broke into the neighbor's house and then broke into ours to just to cover her tracks. How clever. I say all this to show just how effectively drugs can destroy a family. Our neighbors were good people. They would make sure we ate and my mom would often send me to their house to ask for eggs, sugar, bread, or whatever we needed to ensure we were good. What a way to be molded to be "STRONG".

Looking back now I understand that the things my mom endured really messed with her head and caused a lot of her mental issues. Mental health is a serious and real issue that is often ignored in the black community

Chapter 6
The Answered Prayer

My grandmother had to leave work and school constantly to ensure we were taken care of. One day a knock on the door came, and that was rare because our locks didn't work. Everyone on our block knew that they could just walk in our house. It was my grandmother, who had had enough. She decided to take us from my mother. My mom signed the papers with no hesitation.

It was surprising to see my mother even being up. My mother would often sleep for days. Any time she was up, she was gone. I remembered feeling rescued the day that my grandmother came to get my brother and I. When I looked her in the eyes though, I could see they were full of tears and they didn't seem happy.

I vowed right then and there that I would make sure she never cried again. I always wanted her to smile because she was so often sad. It was a totally different world living with grandma. It was a comforting and safe environment but I still wondered how and where my mom was constantly.

Apparently, she got evicted again and this time she was on her own. As I grew, I mostly saw my mom behind bars. I was happy because at least she was safe. There was a peace and comfort that came with her being locked up. I wouldn't have to worry about my mother being harmed by the streets or receiving that devastating call of something happening to her.

I knew even then that being on the streets was not good for my mother. If she wasn't in jail, there was no telling where my mom would be.

CHAPTER 7
The Awakening of an Uproar

I loved my grandmother for rescuing us, but my little brother started acting out. He was filled with so much rage and anger. He only learned destruction and misguidance in his early childhood development. He grew up depressed and often acted out. problem after problem resulted in getting kicked out of school after school. Thankfully, my grandmother never gave up on him. I watched her on her hands and knees praying day and night.

I never wanted to feel like a burden so I never showed any emotion, being strong was all I knew. One day I came home from school to find my baby brother unconscious with a letter saying that it was all too much and he no longer wanted to stay here. He was only 6 at the time.

I panicked and called 911 to save him. They did just that but they also called CPS. To think if only my grandmother wasn't working so hard with no help to put clothes on our bakcs, food on the table, shelter over our heads, and pay the bills [the things we needed to survive] this would have never happened. Even after she took care of all of this it left her with just enough. And of course the government said she didn't need help, you know, the common lie told just so we won't get ahead as a people. I will never understand how a person who paid bills and took care of everything never needed help. But this was a strong black woman, I never saw her break. Looking back, can you imagine her worries, fears, heartbreak, and doubts surrounding her reality?

Time went on while my grandmother was fighting to keep us from the system. The state initially stepped in and my little brother was placed in foster care. The system thought that it would be better, but he only got worse.

He started running away from home after home. The lead paint poisoning and my mother's drug use while he was in her womb really messed with his mind.

Destruction was all he saw from his parents. Not to mention the things that may have happened when no one watched him.

Chapter 8
Brother

My brother, my heart eventually fell into the fast life. That's all he dreamt of. I remember a church member asked him what he wanted to be and he said a gangster. Not a police officer, not a preacher but a "gangsta", and he lived by that. In the 9th grade he dropped out of school and started hustling. He couldn't wait to get out there.

Times had changed. When I was coming up and trying to hustle, the hustlers brought me a pair of tennis shoes and told me to stay in school. They would give me money just to go because they cared. My brother loved it though and stealing cars became his hobby.

At the age of 12 he was already a juvenile delinquent. He didn't know that jails were nothing more than a billion-dollar industry, a future snatcher, a cage not fit for kings and queens. He got himself a gun because it was necessary while running the streets.

One thing he hated was authority. I remember feeling scared for him. This was my little brother, who was going to feed him? Was he Okay?

I started feeling angry. I felt hate knowing that both my mother and my brother were out there and they just left me. How selfish of me to want them to be with me so badly.

Memoirs of Desire

Chapter 9
The Makings of Me

Growing up I had a lot of mixed emotions. I guess you could say I grew up emotional. To be honest, I got so focused on the idea of not becoming like my mom that it became my obsession. I tried so hard to be the strong one, the good one, the honor roll student.

My grandmother raised me with rules, morals, guidance, and stability. All things I wasn't used to when I lived with mom. I raised my brother and myself for almost 12 years essentially by myself. I just wanted my family.

I loved being with my grandmother. She kept us in church on Sundays which was her only day off. My whole life, she always tried her best and did right by the family. She was the nurse to my great grandmother which made me a little nurse too. She would take me to school with her and to work. She wasn't going to lose twice. She did everything in her power to do the right thing.

My grandmother arranged carpools so that I could get to school on time when she had to work nights. I would have to stay overnight at my great grandmother's house. Until one day the same person that molested my mom also tried to do the same thing to me.

It all started to make sense to me, why my mom always asked me if someone had touched me. My advice to everyone is to watch your children because a predator could be right under your nose and you may not even know it.

He did sneaky things like come in my room at night and ask to see my private parts. It was just plain creepy stuff.

For years this went on. I saw myself starting to get attached to women. Women who were much older (like my teachers). At a young age, I felt my teacher was my first woman crush.

We talked on the phone, I wrote her love letters, and then one day I told her about the sexual abuse and she reported it. Until this day I have never thanked her but if she gets the chance to read this I would like to say "thank you" because you saved my life in a way. But at that time, I was mad.

I was mad because I felt embarrassed. It's a shame how society makes you feel dirty for talking about molestation and abuse as if it's your fault that a dirty thing happened. I pray that this generational curse gets broken.

All I can remember was going through a lot after that but I kept it all bottled in. That never stopped me from doing good in school. I liked school,but in the back of my mind all I can remember saying to myself is that I didn't want to be like my mom.

I put all this pressure on myself at such a young age. Time had gone by but my grandmother's rules, morals, guidance, and stability never really changed.

I eventually got my high school diploma early, graduated at 16 and started taking college courses right after. I even signed up to be an addiction counselor. I wanted to change the world.

One day I asked my grandmother if I could stay out until 9:30pm. I started to feel like I didn't want to be that little innocent girl anymore. I had graduated, I felt like I was grown enough to stay out. "I did my chores, I graduated, I'm in college why can't I stay out? You know what, that's okay I'm moving out." … "Ashley if you think you're grown, and you know what the world is all about then I will not stop you."

I always thought it would be a fight, but she never stopped me. Look at me thinking I had it all figured out.

I moved in with who I thought was the love of my life at the time. It was good for the first year meanwhile, my grandmother and I weren't really talking but I always checked in. I hadn't seen my brother or my mother for almost two years.

I figured if I fell in love with a woman, I wouldn't be abused, pregnant, or thought less of. But when you're taught a pattern, you will eventually start doing exactly what you saw. We fought horribly all the time, but I loved her so much I couldn't let her think I couldn't carry my own weight, so I started hustling.

I thought "how ironic", I was trying to be a grown woman with a woman twice my age. I wouldn't dare see us in the dark though, I would have done anything to keep those lights on, the rent paid, and the water on. Some moments I remember feeling lost and out of place.

My partner was more like a mother figure. Boy did I have it all screwed up. This relationship led me to the streets and eventually, I dropped out of school because it didn't pay the bills.

Chapter 10
Mother's Day Devastation

It was all good, that fast life. The money was coming in and I was lucky enough not to be caught. I guess I started getting a little relaxed because one Mother's Day I finally had my mom over who had just gotten released from prison.

"The Ten Crack Commandments" by Biggie Smalls was playing and there was a strange knock on the door. If you're guessing who it was, it was the police. I managed to get the house raided.

I mean if it wasn't a sign that "The Ten Crack Commandments" came on I don't know what would be. Since I hid my stash in my grandmother's nursing clothes, I figured I could take charge for the 3 pills sitting on the mantel but it was too late to grab them.

I thought I had it all figured out. They continued and raided my grandmother's house. Because she thought I would never put her in harm's way, she let the police come in without a warrant.

I realized then just how important it was to know your rights when dealing with the police because even though I was wrong they broke the law to enforce it. I managed to get the entire house arrested including my mom who was clean and was just released on parole.

My family getting locked up on Mother's Day based on my actions hurt me deeply. I was supposed to be protecting my loved ones and here I was putting their freedom at risk.

There are no shortcuts in life. Most of the shortcuts I took became roadblocks. Can you imagine your loved ones and their kids being in all this mess that you caused?

Once I got a record it only got longer. I think my wakeup call was in 2007. I was arrested on Christmas Eve and my mom was arrested again right downstairs from me. Meanwhile, my little brother was down the street in the men's detention center.

I called my grandmother, something I hadn't done since hiding drugs in her home. She said, "All I want is for one of you to make it". Those words crushed me. Can you imagine how she felt? Maybe like a failure…possibly thinking on what she did wrong, when in fact she did nothing wrong.

We were just humans going through this thing called life and making choices. I hated that she blamed herself for our mistakes. But do you know what she did?

She started to pray, something she never ceased to do. That night when dinner came on Christmas, they gave me two pieces of bread and a salad. I think that was the first time in my life I ever cried because my family gatherings always had turkey and everything else that made me feel warm and loved on the holidays.

It takes the smallest things to break you and my thing was food. My mom managed to sneak me some peanut butter crackers, tennis shoes, a polo shirt, and some pants. At that moment I realized how much respect she had in these types of places. She made sure I was good that holiday.

It meant so much to me because I remember feeling protected. She went through so many risks knowing she could get in trouble, but she sacrificed.

That was my mom. At that moment my resentment was gone because I understood, life gives you curveballs and we all try to make the best out of what is thrown at us or we make our own game. I didn't feel alone.

Her presence was so prevalent to me. I think that was the first time I felt that in my life. I got out of that situation and got a little side job, it wasn't much but a start was better than none. All I knew was that I wanted to live but I also realized how much time I had used that destroyed me. The words my grandmother would say to me echoed in my mind.

Chapter 11
The Choice

I was doing so much robbing and hustling. It dawned on me that I didn't have any skills for the work world, only survival skills.

Interview after interview, let down after let down, my relationship was ending. I remember feeling suffocated. Many times, I contemplated suicide, but I always felt like that was for the weak mind and the personality I tried to portray wasn't that, even though I was weak in so many ways. I had to keep up the fake me that I had all together.

I ran, I took my coward self and ran away for "space". I left that relationship and everything that came with it. In reality, I was just running from myself.

A friend let me crash on their couch and for a minute it felt like I had a family. It gave me piece of mind. It felt inviting and safe, but I was losing total control.

I started drinking everyday just because it helped me deal with my harsh realities. I was 20-years old and had nothing to show for it. All I did was party and act promiscuous.

I called it fun when in all actuality I was playing Russian roulette with the devil. Just when you think life will turn one way, there goes those curve balls showing up. I wasn't dodging them; I was actually getting hit and picking up the same traits that I said I never wanted to have. I was becoming the same person I said I didn't want to be like.

I was looking for love, affection, and attention. It dawned on me that I didn't even know how to give the things that I was looking for. And although I wanted love, I wouldn't let anyone get close enough to my heart.

If it felt like there was a little penetration into my heart, I would get paranoid and flee. Being loved and giving love became my biggest fears and my biggest challenges. I made a choice at that moment to close off my heart, too terrified of the unknown.

Chapter 12

The Reunion

Four years had gone past, I was working. I wanted so badly to go back to my grandmother's house which always felt like home, but my pride and ego wouldn't let me.

I never wanted to hear the words "I told you so". But God has a way of showing up because she called me. She told me that she missed me and wanted to see me.

I went back around and knew that my grandmother needed more help now than ever. She was taking care of my great-grandmother who had early-stage dementia and she was getting older herself.

All I thought to myself was "I could have been there". How selfish of me to not be. That same night I lost my great-grandmother who died in my grandmother's arms.

I just promised her we would have a dinner and a movie date the next day. I thought to myself "I just came back into their lives, there was so much wasted time".

If there is someone that you love out there, take it from me, never take the time you have with them for granted. We never know how much time we have with the ones we love. Just when you think you have life all figured out, it will take an unexpected turn that you've never dreamt of.

At that moment I wanted to live free from guilt and shame. But all I did was stick to my same old script because I didn't know how to change or maybe I was too scared to.

Memoirs of Desire

Chapter 13
This Time

This time around would be different. My next companion would be my friend and not a mother figure because no companion wants to raise a child. I'm just learning that now. Partners want to be equal and maybe that's why I sucked at it. I was naïve. It started well, we partied, we did everything together. Life was starting to feel normal. Whatever that is.
I was working to save up to get a car. I moved into a nice duplex with a fireplace and bar. This was far better than what I was used to.

This time I worked for it and I finally had my chance to live. I would succeed, I would control my life and destiny. No one would take anything from me.

I would help everyone in my reach, that became my motto along with, treat others how I want to be treated. I started to travel and see different parts of the world. When I saw those new places in the world, I noticed they were cleaner and nicer.

I didn't even know how to react when a stranger on the street showed more kindness than people I saw every day.

I cried every day when I traveled to the Bahamas because I was happy. I could finally relax, but the funny thing about a vacation is it's only momentary and you eventually must go back to reality.

So, I urge you to live a life where everyday feels like a vacation.

Happiness is the ultimate goal that we all strive for.

I started to help people. I let a good friend of mine move into our home for two weeks because he had fallen on some hard times. It would be a step of working on something God would have wanted which was to be kind to one another.

If you see your fellow brother in a downward spiral, you should help them.

Those two weeks turned into a year and went from feeling like one big happy family to me pulling up at my own home feeling like an outsider. The guy that I was helping was disrespecting me and stabbing me in the back. He was plotting and living like a king on my dime.

He told my companion things I shared with him in confidence along with things that weren't true. Then, he turned around and told me things about her.

I eventually knew I had to leave because I hate to feel uncomfortable. I left them everything and all I took was my clothing.

At that time all I wanted was peace of mind. He became so involved in our business that she didn't believe what I believed and neither did I.

We allowed people and ourselves to destroy our friendship. If you have someone important in your life, learn how to effectively communicate with each other. I have ruined a lot of relationships due to lack of communication.

I shared my food, water, and everything I had with this guy, and he crossed me. One thing that crossed my mind was what makes us think we are better than God when these things happen?

Look at what Judas did to Jesus by betraying Him, that still didn't change the way he loved him though.

In closing, I have realized the way we live life is what makes us unique. We are here to make mistakes. How would we ever grow if we didn't?

Never take anything personal because the one you are looking down on could be you tomorrow. If you do something for someone, expect nothing in return.

That way it won't hurt as bad if there is a letdown in the end. Always remember, if you love someone, love them hard and love them deep because love is really all that matters.

Let's look after one another. Let's try to break the curse of being ashamed of speaking the truth. Most importantly, let's forgive as God forgives us. We are supposed to forgive seventy times seven. There isn't any harm in this type of growth.

If there is something you want to change, change it. You might like it.

This is not the end, but thank you for hearing my beginning. I hope you enjoyed part one of Memoirs of Desire. Please join me for part two that is coming soon. Take this time to reflect and write whatever comes to your mind good, bad, happy, or sad on the journal page.

Prayer

Lord, thank you for the opportunity to gather us here today. I pray that you lead and guide the reader of this book and their hands as they write whatever might be on their heart. I pray they would know and feel that they are loved and thought of. In the name of Jesus, Amen.

Journal

_____

_____

_____

_____

_____

_____

_____

_____

_____

_____

_____

_____

_____

_____

_____

_____

_____

_____

_____

_____

_____

About the Author

Ashley Anderson is a philanthropist, radio personality, author, motivational speaker, CPR instructor, and is the executive director of three assisted living facilities catering to the elderly population. She is extremely dedicated to helping break generational curses of trauma for people of all ages and backgrounds. She is a proud owner of a vacation business called "Vacations Your Way," which she has used to help in the healing process by exposing people to diverse, cultural experiences. She educates on how to save lives and gives back to the community she loves through various community outreach efforts.